MW01286825

PLEASE READ

Carol Matthews

PLEASE READ

Carol Matthews

ISBN: 978-1-66789-088-3

ACKNOWLEDGMENT

I would like to thank my youngest sister Rose Marie Rodgers for encouraging me to continue writing.

I like to thank my best friend Kevin Sharp. He have always been there for me when it matters the most.

Last but not least, My Brother Martin {Marty} Matthews. He has off and on ask me to send him some of my writing.

I would like to thank Book Baby because they have made it possible for some one like me to have my writing in a book.

ABOUT THE AUTHOR

She was born in the 1950's.

She had been self employed via the way of thinking out side of the box.

Her favorite color is clear.

Her favorite word is nothing.

My brother Clyde told me that I have nine lives like a cat.

He said , what I lack in education I had gained in common since.

This is the last years of my nine lives and I am okay with that.

I GOT HER

The devil played in my mothers womb. Nine lived and two where set free. They are somewhere flush down the toilet or wrapped up in a newspaper thrown away with the rest of the garbage. Nine of them are living in the shadows of memories. Memories of her carbonated friends. The memories of how they were divided and conquered. Memories of the taking of pharmaceutical candies that never worked. Memories of being put behind emotional bars that had no key. Remembering the ghost that sat at the end of the bed. Remembering a great mind that was lost. Maybe she had peace in that. She is dead now. Maybe there is peace in that. Family will go to her grave site. They bow their heads, bring flowers and say some fucked up prayer and sing a song or two. I go to the costly spot. I sit at the end of the grave. I think I should have brought a sandwich and something to drink. I know she is not there. I know she didn't belong here. I'm glad she left. The ground cracked and the sky opened for the lady born in 1922. Goodbye Mom.

SOLDIERS OF BULLSHIT

Here they come racing in this place. Dressed in their Sunday's best. They claim to support me to lay my son to rest. All I can see is their mouths moving and moving. They are singing the same damn song. He is in a better place. How you doing? My heart goes out to you. God knows best. If you need me call me. The simulated hugs, the holding of hands. The list are too many.

They drain me. All I can see is their mouth moving and moving. They sit down or stand up to eat. They are asking who made the potato salad ? I have no appetite. My entire body is being fed upon. Sadness, Anger, Blame, Shame and the list are too many. I sat among these soldiers of bullshit. I keep a serene face. I looked for my distant friend. When it was all over he walk in. I asked him, where have you been? He said, I was walking by clear waters. I asked him, what was on his mind ? Time, all you need is time.

THE WIDOW

They come to you like wolves in sheep clothing. They come to you in human form. They are buzzards that circle around you and your children. They are like vultures waiting to feed on the dead. They are like the snakes in the grass. They will change the essence of you. They are a threat to your soul. To the grieving widow I say on to you. Be like a skilled thief in the night. He moves swiftly and quietly. No one knew when the thief came. No one knew when the thief left. No one knows where he went.

SISTER CALLED

Ring, Ring. Ring. Hello. Hey how are you? Angie died. My heart felt like it dropped on the left side of my body. All that is left is anger and sadness, not going in the same order all the time. She just couldn't navigate this mess that we were born into. I wonder how long can I.

All I can do now is cry inside. Just cry inside. Our bodies are made up of a percentage of water. When it becomes full we can cry. Ring . Ring. Ring. Hello. Hey. How are you? Angie died. It was too hard for her to navigate simulated emotions. The love she so desired never existed.

She was alone in that. I have to pretend not to care. I have a headache all over my body. All of us are here on this earth through no fault of our own. Human suffering is no joke. To be sane and insane are the same. To manipulate human suffering with a hug, a hearty laugh and a smile takes a miracle.

DAYS GONE BY

Old now, I am old now. I think I am real old now. Days gone by. Like black ice put out in the blazing hot sun. Art that glides through the hands. A voice that sing songs that echoes in one's mine. A dancer that dance to a saxophone. Like black ice put out in the blazing hot sun. A mathematician, a doctor, a lawyer a builder and the psychological heart healer's. They are like black ice put out in the blazing hot sun. I am old now. I think I am real old now. No one knew. No one noticed. Better to keep it hidden. Better to keep it quiet. Like black ice put out in the blazing hot sun. Days gone by. Why?

NOTHING

I see shadows of the unexplainable. Children playing on invisible streets. A tree that speaks. A sky with no color. People are drinking red water. Rotten hands sharing food from garbage that has been spit out from the sewer. Men smell of perfume. Women smell of mans cologne. A door that whispers to another that is always closed. There is air for sale if you can afford it.

MOM

She slept in a small bedroom that was next to the kitchen. Her room was always kept dark. She would cover the window with news paper and then tack a thick blanket around it. Her bedding was always dirty. She never wore shoes and the bottom of her feet looked as tho she had walked in dirt . I watched her as she got up out of her bed. She walked across the kitchen floor. She smelled of sweat that had dried over from nights before. Her dress was torn and raggedy.

She would open a door that lead to small entrance way and then she would open the door to the outside. She would look up at the night sky. Her gray eyes glaring and glassy. Then she would go into a chant that would become louder and louder. *Ha- Ca- Ma - Sha -Ka.!. Do-Ka- Ma- Da- Ka!. Ha- Ca- Ma- Sha -Ka!. Do- Ka- Ma- Da -Ka!.* The lord is coming! The lord is coming!

She would bounce her bent body from side to side as she chanted. She was sweating profusely. This seem to have went on for hours. We watched her. Helplessly. Finally she would start walking back to her room. She would moan out oh glory, oh glory until she made in back into her bed room. She would lay down in her bed and start to sob. Between her sobbing, she would moan out oh glory, oh glory until she went to sleep.

MOM & ME

I am the black sheep of my family and that well runs deep.
Sometimes I'm lonely.

It is only in my heart. The one that I wear on my sleeve. Thats
my art of acceptance. I will not swallow pain. I will digest it.
Listening to my mom's loud chanting of *Ha-Ca-Ma-Sha-Ca!.
Do- Ca- Ma-Da-ka!.* The lord is coming! The lord is coming!
I screamed out even louder. Tears of sadness and anger rolled
down my face. How could you let yourself get in this place?
These out burst is of your own guilt and shame. This is you
looking for someone else to blame. This is your own self pity.
This is the shit thats left over from what the toilet paper missed.
Wash your hands! Just wash your hands! There is no *Ha- Ca-
Ma- Sha -Ca!.* There is no *Do -Ka- Ma- Da- Ca!.* There is no
lord is coming! It was only you that tried to find love in the
arms of twisted minded men. It was only you that gave your
flowers to the unholy. What a fucked up duty. You lost your
beauty. Now we all have to pay? Misdirection of your affection.
Thinking about her dirty feet. She kicked me out in the Street.
Now the sky is my blanket. The concrete my bed. At night the
stars gave me light. I like it better here.

A HOLY GHOST

Only the Almighty can guide me. The Angels that he sends to me whisper in my ear.

The Angels speak to me in my dreams. It is all in the spiritual soul of me. Anger, grieve, frustration and all things that break my spirit are not my own. That cannot be the rock of my soul of souls. No it cannot. So that has been written. So that has been told. I am not here for that. I am here to feel the wind. I am here to look up at the sky that covers us all. I am here to be loved. I am here to love. That's the challenge. Only the Almighty can guide me. The angels hug me. A mortal man can not give such an embrace.

EVICTION

What do you know, I am an embryo. I am growing. Sounds
I hear from inside and out. I really don't know what they're
talking about. Finally shadows, colors blue red and yellow's.
I find this house I share with another fellow. Yes, I am a twin
my short term friend. His life will end before it begin. I got
an idea now that I can feel my hands and my feet. This will be
neat. Just the right tools for painting. Flipping and flopping
all around, ignoring the inside and outside sound. I had to
get my painting done. No time to play. I want to finish my
work sometime today. I will fix up this place. It's starting to
look good. Just in a little while I will be proud. Maybe I will
stay a year or two, especially with all the work I had to do. The
sounds outside are getting really loud. Some one said push
and push and they are out. Some one said happy birthday! No
way! My birthday? This is a strong arm eviction. I did not get
due process of the law. I was going to live here for a couple of
years. I would cry but I had no tears. Some one is squeezing
my head. My exit would be a bloody bed. I will fight to stay
in my home. I going to sue. This is what I will have to do. I
am upside down, I refuse to breathe. I was flipped around so
fast they skinned my littles knees. Some one will have hell to
pay and I will make sure its before judgement day. I hold my
mouth tight, this time they will see this little body can fight.
Out of no where I felt extreme pain. This abuser is totally
insane. He slapped me on my behind. The thrust went up my
little spine. I couldn't hold back any longer I started to cry.
Oh my little body shaken up inside. I could tell this was not

going to end well. A rat and roach infested house is where I was gonna stay. I couldn't run then but I plan to get away. I heard a loud and strong voice yell, welcome to the world girl! I'll see you another day. That is when the welfare pay and then he went away.

In the womb I was given a few talents and one of them was art. Destitution was my canvas but it will not be until death do us part.

INVISIBLE

Here I am holding the hand of my invisible twin brother. We walked down a half a block and we seen a small house. We went up to the door and I knocked. There was all of our sibling and all of our kin. They ignored us when we walked in. Their thoughts were else where. We spoke out loud but no one heard us. Too painful to acknowledge. Better to ignore. We walked out the door. Some one closed it behind us. Just disgust. This we already knew. They were told that we are the retard and the crazy. It started to pour down rain and hail. The sharp cold ice felt like razors grazing against our skin. There's no place for shelter. Nothing is worst than having no mercy. Miles from no place in which we came. Bright shining stars that wrapped around the sun. The stars reached out like two large hands to embrace us and the Sun gave us warmth. This is the place our new life begin. In this place we have family and friends. We are Invisable no more.

ABANDONMENT

They was told I would be this way before I was born. Developmentally disabled and I am deformed. That is where the pressure was put on. The decision was made and now they are all gone. Right to life protesters said let him be born anyway. My parents will be too old to take care of me one day. They mortgage their homes to keep me in place. When the money was used up they took me away. I live in a state ran nursing home that's where I'll stay. The Aids are tired short staffed every day. The smell of the hidden filth and human waste will make the best of them run out of this place. Just take a look at all of our faces. You know how it is in these state ran places. No need to come it will be a heart breaking visit. Your time will be wasted. All that's left is despair and you can taste it. The state just don't care. I am slumped over in my chair and there is old dried up food in my hair. Never make a complaint I wouldn't dare. The only thing I can pray for is to die tonight. If I could suffocate that will be all right. I do not want to live through this another day. I just want this pain to go away. The pro-life folks they just don't understand. I'm labeled a freak of nature, I'm not a man. They have a Wife. A life that I never had. I heard that some of them are now proud mom's and dads. Right to life protesters won't let me come live with them. When they are confronted they say I can't take care of him!

I'm not so much to criticize but there is one thing I know. To love me and then leave me is not the way to go.

LEARNED TO WALK ON WATER

I was born in an out house. Some think it's funny some think it's sad. I barely knew my Mom and I didn't know my Dad. A beginning like that I was set up to fail. Just a young girl child , I knew my life was hell. Liars, deceivers, thieves and beggars. To top that off was the child molesters. I learned about all of them they thought they where clever. Just concentrated ignorance. Never, never , never. A beginning like that I was set up to fail. I could have been a hooker or put in jail. This is not the way that I was going to live. I reached for a higher power, something got to give. Like hell and back this is what I did. I learned to walk on water. They all ask me how did someone like you manage to do so well? Thanks to all of you son of a bitches I've learned very well. I see you are a homeless mother fucker and the streets are where you belong. I will not treat you as you did me. Stomping and kicking me down. I'm just going to leave you where you are, in the lost and never found. Cause I am walking on water. The liars, deceivers, thieves, and beggars. The top that off was the child molesters. The scum of the earth and they thought they where clever. Just concentrated ignorance. Never, never, never. Who you are and where you come from may not have given you a clue, but don't let no damn body tell you what you can't do. Especially with all the bull shit that they sent you through. Learn to walk on water. Walk on water.

TO BE YOUNG AGAIN

Only if I could be young again! No. Oh no. Not me my friend. Never would I want to be in the age of the trusting innocence. I would never want to be in the state of total shock and surprise. I would never want to believe the unbelievable. Believing in the horrific lies of my elders. They are the ones that are afraid of getting old. That's why they seek the innocence to destroy their souls. They give out destructive advice, it goes on and on until you're gone. The only hope that they had, was to become *Dorian Gray*. They don't understand that was just a movie. They are the offspring of adulterated foolishness. To be young again. No. Not me my friend. Never would I want to live through migraine headaches, heartaches and uncountable disappointments. Totally unaware of the traps. Totally unaware of dangers that were every where. Locked up in places that use pharmaceutical weapons of mass distortion. Locked up because I was the last accident of my mother and father. Post traumatic syndrome? Ha! It haunted me for decades. Candy, cookies and liquor, the gift that was given after child molestation. Unwanted pregnancies after a desperate relationships. Liquor and more Liquor for self medication and sedation.. Oh! I had to find somewhere to go. Out of my mind. Yes, thats it! Out of my mind. I couldn't believe what I was seeing, this can't be human being. Being What? People two and three times my age digging a grave for a teenage mother and her child. What happened to them? They are full of unforgivable, unspeakable sins. I thought that they were my friends. Anyone that comes in contact with them will have to die if they want to rise again. No, no. I would not want to be young again. Digging and crawling through all that slimy and rotten souls of a people. The twisted man made ghetto that are the homes for the born abortions. To live among them is more than a mess. There is no rest. No rest. No rest. My tears like concrete have cemented into my face. I see the old hard lines that have been left behind. These old hard lines I do not mind for me it is a miracle. I learned to be the teacher of myself. I learned to see with tunnel vision. Insisting that I will not be a part of none of these barbaric behaviors. Grabbing at anything that should have always been kept good. Embracing people, a place and things that no one wanted or cared about. It was hard to do so. The hideous truth was mind. I owned it. I found it. An open palm and a closed fist. I got it! I got it!. I am an old lady older than my years and I am finally free. Me. To be young again. No not me my friend, this is the happiest sad I have ever been.

TALKING TO MY FRIENDS

Honor thy mother and father, that's not normal that's divine. The norm is to sleep in my childhood bed. Just tolerating them. Just buying time for you to rest in peace. What's in the fridge? I wanted something to eat. I don't know what goes on in these old people heads. I will inherit this house when they both drop dead. Dad, cover your mouth when you sneeze and hand over the car keys. Just hold your breath. Don't breathe. They have Doctors appointments tomorrow that I will discard. Dealing with all this senile makes my life too hard. That's not normal that is divine. Giving up twenty four hours in my day, watching them rotting away. Hear what I say. They should have made other arrangements any way. I owe them nothing. All of my siblings say the same thing. The won't answer when their telephones ring. Having children is for the wealthy, I did not ask for this poor life you dealt out to me. You have circled your hold life around us, never creating something of your own. You thought we would not put you in a nursing home? That's not normal. That's Divine. We are not the father, the son and your holy ghost. What's really going on here? You want a host? That's not normal, That's Divine. Now that they are dead, we will eat of their bread. We all have what we wanted. Nothing. Mom and Dad is done with their suffering. I wish Mom and Dad was still alive. I would put my selfish ways aside. Too late now, I am all alone. I go to the cemetery. I look at a stone. That's normal, that's divine.

A BROKEN HEART

I want you to say that you are sorry. Sorry for all the lies that you told on me. I want you to say you are sorry for all the lies that followed with your followers. little do you know they knew me. They supported your lies for their own agenda. Their self worth is none. I want you to embrace what sorrow feels like. I want you to know, I had fallen into a bottomless pit. My head hidden like a turtle in its shell. I want you to know, I was waiting for an echo of peace that never came. It is none of my business any more and for that I am grateful. Grateful to understand the ungrateful. I want you to know when one fall so low and think that all hope is gone that is not a given. Where there is life there is hope. I just want you to be happy sometime.

THE GUILTY CONSCIOUS

Don't worry if my mouth is wide open and my eyes rolled back in my head. Take a good guess motherfucker, that means that I am dead. Don't know if there are hanks. Don't know if there are Ghost, but I do know one thing that's what you should hope for the most.

WIND

I am a soldier of life. Too bad I was born that way. The more you know the more it hurts. Too bad I know that is true. I am a soldier that have no Armor, not even a water pistol. Damn. I fought many battles. The wars of pyrrhic victory's. I have never came out unscathed. There is a knock at my door. I open it just to be greeted with an iron fist. I buckled. I fall to my knees. I was able to stand up with the help of a near by chair. I looked into a mirror seeing no reflection. I told myself you can't win this time. I got dress. It is time to ascend into the everlasting. Okay. No choices. My request is to become wind.

FAT

I have a hunger in me that I can't touch. That is why I eat so much. My woman told me that I have many skills. I want her to shut up. I have chicken and fries to kill. Talent I am, I don't give a damn. I'm thinking of peanut butter and a mountain of jam. She said I have to get off disability because I'm too big for her to carry. I know that she loves me but she will never marry. Back to the refrigerator, I know that's insane but working every day cause too much pain. Just love that eating. I'm getting fatter and fatter. The french toast with the real thick batter. Oh, that syrup dripping down the sides, make a man like me feel happy inside. I can't keep doing this job either way I'm going to die. I got to get back on SSI. This woman said keep working. I held in a cry. Huffing and puffing I am lagging behind. Trying to keep a super size sandwich off my mind. I can't keep working for these pennies and dimes. I need to find a chair to rest my behind. Self employment that has once been. I helped her with that only because I am her friend. I mostly watched Tv and I ate. I loved that self employment. That was great. I need to collect that check. This is a do or die. I have no other choice. I will reapply. Direct deposit is where it use to go. Oh how I miss that check that I have no more. She don't understand. I'm just a fat man. I am trying not to do the best I can. Out the door I go to this worthless job. All I can do now is sigh and sob. Talent I am , I don't give a damn. I want a triple decker sandwich boiled eggs and spam. I have a hunger in me that I can't touch. That is why I eat so much.

REALLY

I hope you live to be 110, after all the work you put in. Jumping over hurdles and running track. Running away from a pit bull attack. Who knows where your mind was at. You criticize other's that are not as thin as you. You think it will make it all better. You know that's not true. Look at me! I am sky diving! Oops. I am tangled up in a tree. That didn't hurt me. I only scraped one knee. I look at how they all marvel at me when I cross my skinny legs. I'll go take a shower and then I'll go to bed. Now I lay me down to sleep. I pray to the lord I want eat. I am hungry , famish, I feel so sad. The things I have no control of just make me mad. Starvation is what I can do. Give me strength Oh lord to see the night through. Donuts and pizza thoughts roll around in my head. I will drink a glass of water instead. I see a skeleton of a person when I'm in bed. I lost so much weight, I have no booty cheeks. When I bend over I hear a crunch and a squeak. Now I lay me down to sleep. I pray to the lord that I want eat.

I WANT

I want to be some where that I'm not in it. Twenty is the speed limit and twenty five if you are in a hurry. I want to be in a place where taking a walk is always at a slow pace. Stopping as you go. Just to say hello. To say how are you and really mean it. I want to eat anything and never get fat. I want to smoke a cigarette that won't cause cancer. I want a head that never aches, money that I don't need to spend. I want an entire world of reversible sins. I want to not want anything.

DATING GAME

I am in the dating game. I have studied forensics in my early years and private investigation has always sparked my interest. My personality is one with my studies and my interest. I am locked and loaded. Got to be careful. Got to protect one's self. A date! My first date in years. He called me on my cell phone. I met him at a nice restaurant. I got there early. I watched him as he walked in. He is well dressed, well groomed and his body molded from the gym. My first thought was maybe I could like him. Our conversation was just questions and answers. He did not say much. I got a gut feeling that he was out of touch. Time went by, he called me again. I thought this might be a possible friend. He invited me to his home. Everything had its place and every place had it's thing. My eyes indiscreetly moved around the room. What stood out was the silver spoon. What kind of shit is this? A case of full-blown nepotism. He never kept a job. Just a well dress slob. His mother is his wife and his father has deep pockets. He poured me a glass of his self-pity. I couldn't drink it. This will be a waste of my time. He wanted to mess with my mind. He is a counterfeit of a man. Too bad he will never grow up in this china doll of a house. I am locked and loaded. I ghosted him.

PATHETIC

Oh No! here we go. The Ghetto Gigolo. He lift up her skirt to get in her purse. One dollar, two dollars, and some change. Now that's an N word for you. He runs from pillar to post. Just a low level Con man. A smile and a long embrace as he winks at your girlfriends. One is a nurse, another teacher and the other a social worker. He scopes for the ones with a degree. They all graduated with a minus c. Easy Pickens. One bought him a used car. It didn't go too far. He drove it around the block and it stopped. Another sold her run down home. That one he chose to marry. Now she is a middle-age woman left alone with a baby she now carries. He is a sperm donor of ten. Some are in jail and the bondsman do not accept food stamps. Oh no here we go! The Ghetto Gigolo. Now he is an old man with a dick in his hand. Prostate cancer and testicular too. Have to cut off those testes, nothing else they can do. Good thing we all can say, that the Ghetto Gigolo got his day. And that's an N word for you.

THE SAME

There is worlds in side this world. Do you know which one you're born in? Your race, class, gender and much more than that. Got to live in the world you are in. To venture out is at your own risk. Sometimes it works. Sometimes it don't. Altho, these worlds have somethings in common. They all sleep under the same blanket. The sky. They all go to sleep and don't wake up. They die.

THEY CALL ME JUST A

My name is Justa. I am just a single parent. Just a part of societies under class. I am just a Waitress. They tell me to make sure I get the order right. They look me up and down without giving eye contact. They are laughing and talking and making corporate jokes. They tell me the food was good. They wipe their mouths and blow their noses on the cloth napkins. They left me a fifty cent tip. I am just a Cleaning lady. I am an immaculate cleaner. They shoot balls of paper in the waste paper baskets. They miss. Paper balls all over the floor. They asked me to pick them up. They tell me there is a cobwebs in the corner of the doorstop. I can't see it. I get down on my knees and I go through the motions of using a dust cloth. Sometimes they say thank you. I am just a Personal Care Worker, the lady is in a wheelchair. I scrub and sanitize the wheelchair. I put her on the toilet. I transfer her to the shower. She is dead weight. I have to be careful to do the perfect transfer. She is all clean now. The family say that's a good gal you got there! They say they don't make shit wipers like that anymore. I go to clean the bathroom. Her husband follows me. He ask me can he sneak a feel. My name is Justa . I am Just A Child of God.

SAVE MY SOUL

I walk threw the shadows of death, I fear evil. I am caught between a Lamborghini and a Bentley. When I am released I will truly die.

DR. VISIT

Do you feel safe at home? Are you depressed? Most of us live on planet earth. I am not delusional. I see what they do. I see how it's done. They have separated us all. They have separated the sky. It is now in pieces. I've had systematically induced plastic surgery. I would smile but it makes my face hurt. I would give a hug but I don't want to bring bedbugs to my home. Cockroaches are better. Countless shootings and killings are broadcast on TV. Legalize murders are always forgiven. I live on planet earth. I am not delusional. **Do you feel safe at home? Are you depressed?** I live in the suburbs. I am not delusional. Only cost a dime to invest in a white collar crimes. Hello John, hello Joe, and hello to people that I don't know. Pharmaceuticals are running rampant. My wife walks around in a coma. I tuck my daughter into bed. I kiss and hug her. I say good night. I turn off the lights. She's afraid of the dark. My son knows where to find the good drugs. The ones of my own making. It was never meant to be for him. It was meant for them. Countless murders and deaths that are not being broadcast on TV. I live among the corporate world, the undercover serial killers and people are buried in the basement. I live in the suburbs. I am delusional. I feel safe at home.

DOROTHY JEAN

Sister is one year older than me. She looked at my feet and laughed. She asked me do your feet hurt? I always wore my shoes on the wrong foot. I always had my shoelaces untied. I always made myself comfortable being uncomfortable. I always made myself comfortable being untied. She bent down and said let me see. She taught me how to tie my shoes. She taught me how to put them on the right foot. She said, now don't you feel better? I couldn't tell the difference. Here I go again. Mom would always ask me what time is it? Carol Ann what time is it! Go and see what time is it. I was always afraid of that big Clock. All those numbers on the big scary clock. What time is it? What time is it? I don't know, I can't figure it out. I can't figure it out. Too many numbers. Too many things to think about in one place. Tick Tock. Tick Not. Tick Block. I don't know what time it is. What's the big deal about the time? I am always late. I am always too early. I may not show up at all. What time is it? Ask Dorothy!

DEPRESSION

I have felt so bad I was crying inside and out. Tears ran down my throat to the point I felt like I was being water boarded. I have cried so hard my eyes felt like a waterfall that was on fire. My heart beat felt like an African drummer on steroids. Now here today and the day before that, I am happy. I can't believe it. I am grateful for almost everything. Can't believe it. Incredible. My facial features have always been stony. I looked in the mirror and the refection had a smile on it's face. I thought it was someone else. I stepped away, and looked again. It was me. With a smile. That is Scary.

BREATHE

You are carrying around dead things. Stop that. I can smell you. Too carry around a corpse will produce a horrible smell. You are caring around dead things. Can this be a reproduction of your lack of worth? You like to flash your money, diamonds, cars and all of your things that have no real value. You have become an insecure bragger that have sold yourself out for what you proceed to be the better things in life. That's more than painful. You have committed financial suicide for dead things. You cannot breathe life into what is dead already. It was dead when you got it. It will be dead when you die. It never belong to you anyway. Lay down that burden. Hold a friends hand and walk barefoot in the sand. Take a deep breath and breathe.

IGNORAMUS

They are the consumers, most of what they see on TV. Making their lives harder than what it has to be. Living like a fool. Spending dollars when it's worth a dime. Going to check cashing places all the time. They will invest in low level crimes. Living like a fool. Satisfying valueless wants over their needs. They chose I can't do it , over I will try. When they open their mouth out pops a lie. They use a flash light before turning on the lights. They wear sandals in the winter snow. They wash in recycled soap. They hold close to the cuff, thinking someone want to take there stuff. Their thinking have no meaning. Just living like a Fool.

NIGHTMARE DISORDER

I went to bed angry. I went to sleep. I had a fight. I was choking someone. I stuck my fingers in both of his eyes. I punch him. When he leaned forward , I slapped him as hard as I could in both of his ears. I slapped him with the palms of my hand. Pow! pow! and pow! again. Was bobbling and weaving like a prize fighter. I had him down. The final blow would be with my elbow. I jumped up and slam down on him. Elbow to the chest. What happen?

Somethings choking me! Ouch ! Ouch ! my elbow is throbbing. I think it's broken. Excruciating pain. I woke up on the floor. A sheet was wrapped around my neck. I was sweating . I had a rapid heart beat. Pain all over my body. My queen size bed was now a twin size. I laid on the floor trying to collect myself before calling the paramedics. I realized I was fighting a nightmare. Please listen to me. Do not go to bed angry. It may cause unexplainable property damage. The self-inflicted injuries that will be hard to heal. The never ending hospital bills. It can become quite costly. Quite costly.

THINK

There is a Rat among us. It is being fed by the powers that be. It's irrational to think we can fight that. This Rat need to be eradicated. Rationally thinking. Overindulge the Rodent. That thing will eat anything. Just wait, wait. It might have a fatal heart attack. Wait ,wait. That might take too long. Wait, wait. Get the Cats. The pussies will kill him.

WEDDING & FUNERALS

Weddings and Funerals are one end in the same. To invite family and friends you have nothing to gain. They are all sitting around with a tight pasty grin, glaring in your face. They are all betting on your divorce date. Here they come again. This time with a fake frown. Asking why is she buried in her wedding gown.

GROW UP

A Bible verse: 1 corinthians 13:11. It states, when a child we act as a child. When we become adults we are to put away childish things. You do not have to be a particularly religious person to believe that. When a person becomes an adult they will put away childish things.